Sports Stars

Jen Green

Published by **Atebol Cyfyngedig**, Fagwyr Buildings, Llandre, Aberystwyth, Ceredigion, SY24 5AQ
01970 832 172
www.atebol.com
www.ateducationalbooks.com

ISBN: 978 1 909666 59 7

Project Managers: Dafydd Saunders Jones, Megan Elizabeth Tye
Editor: Gill Matthews
Design: Ceri Jones Studio, stiwdio@ceri-talybont.com
Picture Research: Dafydd Saunders Jones and Megan Elizabeth Tye
Published with the financial support of the Welsh Books Council
Printed by Cambrian Printers, Aberystwyth, Ceredigion

Photographs: Alamy Images, Getty Images (cover)
Alamy Images: pp 2/3, 4/5, 6/7, 10/11, 12/13, 14/15, 16/17, 20/21, 24/25, 26/27, 28/29
Getty Images: pp 2/3, 4/5, 8/9, 10/11, 12/13, 14/15, 18/19, 22/23, 24/25, 26/27, 28/29

Acknowledgements
Atebol wishes to thank Jen Green for her professionalism during the preparation of these resources. We would also wish to thank all individuals mentioned in this book for their support and enthusiasm in being part of this exciting project.

Contents

Sporting excellence

Introduction

From rugby to athletics, boxing, football and cycling, Wales has a long and proud tradition of sport that stretches back decades. We feature just some of the greatest modern sporting heroes, but there are many, many more.

What's your sport?

From golf to gymnastics, darts to diving, sports of every kind are played in Wales. Whether you like your sport fast and furious or ice-cool and deadly accurate, there is a sport to suit every taste. Sport also offers you the chance to have fun, build key skills, stay fit and make new friends. So get down to the nearest gym or sports centre and get stuck in!

Sport Wales

Sport Wales is the organisation responsible for encouraging sport in Wales. Log on to www.sportwales.org.uk/. The aim is to get - yes, everyone - hooked on sport for life! Their mission is to support athletes at every level: "From grassroots sport to the Millennium Stadium, we want to develop a nation of champions."

Disability Sport Wales

If you are into sport and have a disability, Disability Sport Wales is your first point of contact. See www.disability-sport-wales.org. This organisation aims to develop sporting opportunities for anyone with a disability. If you stick with it you could even become a Paralympian and compete at the highest level.

Key contacts

Sport Wales has a list of clubs for every sport in every area. If watersports are your thing, check out the Plas Menai National Watersports Centre, Caernarfon, at www.plasmenai.co.uk/. Other key contacts are given throughout this book.

Summer of sport

At the London Olympics and Paralympics Welsh and Team GB athletes proved their skills as they scooped 185 medals. At a home celebration in Cardiff Bay, First Minister Carwyn Jones said: "Inspirational, heroic and awe-inspiring… They rightly deserve to be called our greatest team."

Do you really want to be a sports star?
Go to page 30 to find out!

Posting gold

The Royal Mail celebrated British achievement in the 2012 Olympics and Paralympics by painting a postbox gold in the home town of every gold-medal winner. Wales has seven gold postboxes: in Wrexham (home of rower Tom James), Cardiff (cyclist Geraint Thomas), Flint (Jade Jones, taekwondo) and in Bridgend, Hay-on-Wye, Swansea and Tredegar in honour of Paralympic athletes Aled Davies, Josie Pearson, Ellie Simmonds and Mark Colbourne.

Cycling, swimming...

Champion cyclists Nicole Cooke, Geraint Thomas, Mark Colbourne and Becky James have raised the profile of cycling. The home of Welsh cycling is the National Velodrome, Newport, see www.newport.gov.uk/activeNewport/index.cfm/velodrome. Paralympic athlete Ellie Simmonds has inspired a generation of swimmers. The Wales National Pool in Swansea (www.walesnationalpoolswansea.co.uk/) is the nation's top pool.

FOOTBALL

Gareth Bale

The Wales and Real Madrid winger is classed among the world's top footballers. Speed, skill and stamina – Gareth has it all.

Did you know?

Gareth's sternest critic is his dad, Frank, who works as a school caretaker. Gareth says: "He always told me off if I did something wrong. Even now he still does it. But he makes me get better and I want to keep proving him wrong in order to keep him quiet."

Profile

Name:	Gareth Bale
Born:	16 July 1989 in Cardiff
Career:	Raised in Cardiff, Gareth signed for Southampton FC in 2005 at the age of 16. He moved to Tottenham Hotspur two years later. He now plays for Real Madrid in Spain.

Big break

Gareth caught the eye of Southampton FC playing six-a-side football at the age of nine. Once at Southampton he started making a name for himself as a free kick specialist. In May 2007 he moved to Premier League team Tottenham Hotspur and scored in his second game. Up until then, Gareth had played left back, but Spurs manager Harry Redknapp moved him to a more attacking position as a winger. The gamble soon paid off as Gareth began scoring goal after goal. Gareth has recently started playing for the Spanish team Real Madrid, who paid an astronomical £83.5 million for him!

Scoring for Wales

Gareth made his debut for Wales in May 2006 at just 16. A few months later he became Wales' youngest ever goal-scorer when he curled in a free-kick against Slovakia.

Why does Gareth stand out?

Former Spurs manager Harry Redknapp says: "He's an amazing player. He's got everything. There's not a weakness in his make-up."

Football expert Mark Lawrenson says: "He is one of the quickest players I've ever seen. He has the ability to perform and use his technique at great pace."

Insider info

So what is the secret of Gareth's goal-scoring success? "It's hard to explain what I do. You just keep practising... but do I know what the ball is going to do? No – I haven't a clue!"

Honours board

2009 Named Wales Footballer of the Year
2010 Voted BBC Wales Sports Personality of the Year
2010/11 Named Professional Footballers' Association (PFA) Player of the Year
2010/11, 2012/13 PFA Players' Player of the Year
2012/13 Named Football Writers' Association Footballer of the Year

Martial arts expert Jade Jones won Britain's first ever gold medal in taekwondo in the 2012 Olympics. The whirlwind from Flint was just 19 at the time.

Jade Jones

"What drives me? Olympic gold – to be the very best. And to make my friends and family proud."

Did you know?

Jade's grandfather introduced her to taekwondo when she was eight years old to "keep her out of trouble". He supported her early fighting career.

Profile

Name:	Jade Jones
Born:	21 March 1993 in Bodelwyddan, Denbighshire
Lives:	Flint
Career:	Educated at Flint High School. Jade left at 16 to pursue her sport, and joined the GB Taekwondo Academy based in Manchester. Competing weight: 57 kg (130 lb).

Big break
Key match: 9 August 2012 - final of the 57 kg category at the London Olympics
Opponent: Yuzhuo Hou of China
What happened? After a cautious opening round Jade went on the attack, gaining a 5-1 lead. Her opponent fought back but Jade held on to win the contest 6-4.

Insider info
Taekwondo means "way of striking with feet and fists". Taekwondo originated in Korea as a blend of karate and a traditional Korean martial art. It became an Olympic sport in 2000.

Honours board
2010 Took bronze at the Junior World Championships in Mexico
2010 Won gold at the Youth Olympic Games in Singapore
2011 Won gold in 62 kg category at the US Open, her first senior title
2011 Won silver at the World Championships in South Korea
2012 Took gold in 57 kg category at London Olympics
2013 Awarded MBE for services to sport

Training tips
The 2013 World Championships took place in Mexico at 2100 m above sea level. Preparation for the event involved sleeping in a specially built altitude centre. "Sleeping and training at altitude was really hard to begin with, but it really helped us to prepare for the competition."

Revenge is sweet!
Jade's Olympic win over Yuzhuo Hou was revenge for her defeat by the Chinese fighter at the 2011 World Championships. Her key ambition is to win gold again at the Rio Olympics in 2016.

Ellie Simmonds

"Coming second is not an option."

Big break
- At 13, Ellie was the youngest member of the British team at the Beijing Olympics and Paralympics.
- The same year, 2008, she won BBC Young Sports Personality of the Year – the youngest athlete ever to win.
- At 14, she became the youngest person ever to get the MBE.

Insider info
Ellie has achondroplasia – a type of dwarfism. The 1.2 m (4 ft) athlete swims freestyle over 50 to 400 metres. She competes in the S6 class. S means freestyle, while the numbers 1-10 stand for levels of disability, where 10 is least severe.

Did you know?
Ellie trains in the Wales National Pool, Swansea. She does nine two-hour sessions a week. Her only day off is Sunday! When not training, Ellie is studying for her AS levels.

The secret of Ellie's success? "The main thing is to enjoy it. If you don't enjoy what you do you don't give everything and you don't get the best out of it."

Profile
Name:	Eleanor May Simmonds
Born:	11 November 1994 in Walsall, England
Career:	Moved to Swansea when she was 11 to use the city's world-class swimming pool.

Teen swimming sensation Ellie Simmonds is one of Britain's most popular athletes. She won two golds at the 2008 Paralympic Games. At London 2012 her haul was two golds, a silver and a bronze.

Ellie is known for:

- her big grin and sunny nature
- crying with happiness after winning gold at the Beijing Paralympics

Honours board

2008 Two golds in the Beijing Paralympics, for the 100 m and 400 m freestyle S6

2008 Won BBC Young Sports Personality of the Year

2009 Awarded MBE

2009/10 Ellie won gold in ten World Championship events, and five at European Championship events. She also broke eight world records

2012 In the London Paralympics, Ellie successfully defended her 400 m title, smashing the world record by 5 seconds. She also won gold in the 200 m individual medley, silver in the 100 m and bronze in the 50 m

2013 Awarded OBE for services to Paralympic sport

2013 Won a further 3 golds at the World Championships

RUGBY

Sam Warburton

Rugby star Sam Warburton led Wales to victory in the 2011 Six Nations Tournament. A superb sprinter and ultra-tough tackler, he is seen as one of the best flankers in the game.

Big break

2009 was Sam's breakthrough year. He was selected to play for the Cardiff Blues and for Wales in the same year. His first game for Wales was against the USA.

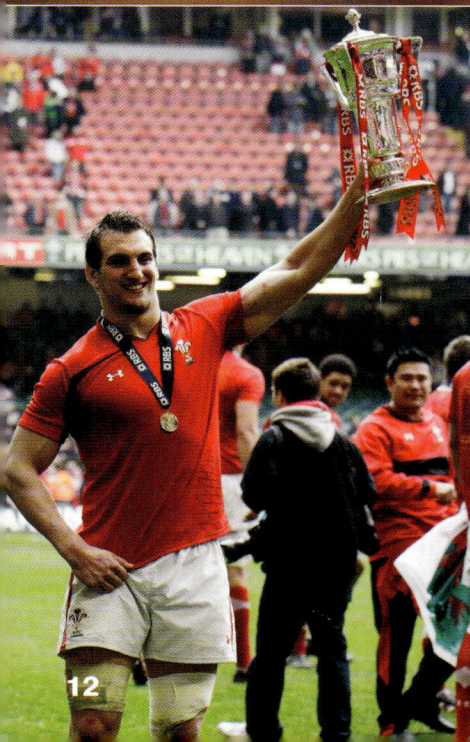

Profile

Name:	Sam Warburton
Born:	5 October 1988 in Cardiff. Grew up in Whitchurch, north Cardiff, where his father is a fireman
Career:	Began his career at Glamorgan Wanderers before moving to the Cardiff Blues in 2009
Position:	Openside flanker

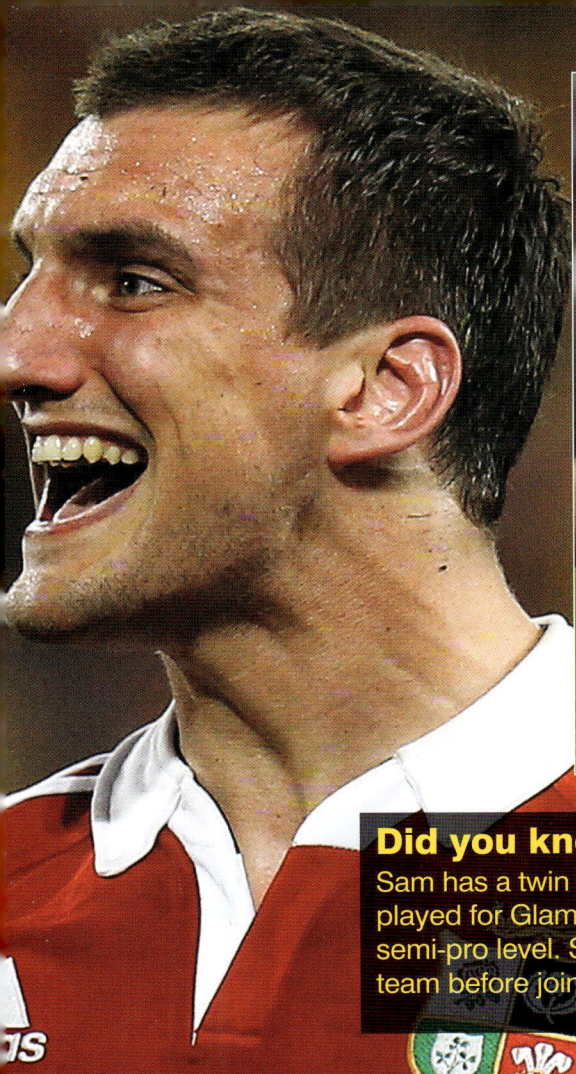

Did you know?

Sam has a twin brother, Ben, who played for Glamorgan Wanderers at a semi-pro level. Sam played for the same team before joining the Cardiff Blues.

Honours board

2009 Made debut for Wales
2011 Scored his first international try against Italy in the Six Nations tournament
2011 Led Wales to victory in the Six Nations. Also captained Wales for the World Cup
2012 Led Wales in the Six Nations again despite injuries
2013 Captained British and Irish Lions tour to Australia

Leading Wales and the Lions

From an early age Sam was a natural choice as captain. He led the Wales Under-18s, Under-19s and Under-20s. He skippered the Wales senior squad for the first time in June 2011 at the age of 22. This made him Wales' second-youngest captain ever, after Gareth Edwards, who led the team at 20 in 1968. In 2013 he was named captain for the British and Irish Lions tour to Australia – the youngest ever Lions captain at 24.

Insider info

So what's it like to skipper older and more experienced players? "The first worry I had was not coming across as patronising to the senior players. The coaches say it doesn't matter how old you are."

Inspiration

Sam's role model is Cardiff Blues team-mate Martyn Williams, a classic openside flanker who is Wales' most capped player. Martyn has represented Wales 100 times and also played for the British Lions. Sam says: "I'm still watching tapes of Martyn."

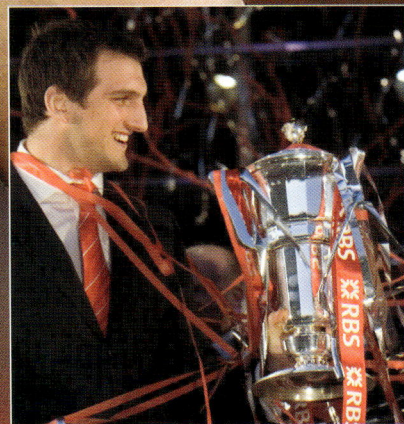

Motorbike racer Chaz Davies is no stranger to the fast lane! In 2011 he became the first Welshman to win the World Supersport Championship. He also won the BBC Wales Sports Personality of the Year.

Long struggle

Chaz's 2011 win in the World Supersport Championship came after years of hard grind. After his junior racing debut in 1999 he progressed to 125 cc and then 250 cc bikes – the youngest rider ever to do so. But then came years of having to switch teams and competitions to get a ride on a top-notch bike. Looking back he says: "I'm glad in some ways that I had to go through it as it's made me realise how precious success really is." He made his debut in the Moto GP series in 2007.

Golden year: Big break

In his golden 2011 season Chaz competed in the World Supersport Championship on a Yamaha bike. The 12-race series began badly when a tyre problem forced him out of the first race. But he went on to win six races and also took a second and third place. His overall triumph made him only the second Briton to win the championship since it began in 1997.

Insider info

The Supersport Championship is one below the top-flight World Superbikes Championship. Winning the Supersport title on a Moto GP bike gained Chaz promotion to Superbikes. The new class took a while to get used to. What's the difference? Chaz says: "Moto GP bikes are machines especially built for nothing but track racing. The bike equivalent of a Formula 1 car. A Superbike is much more like a tuned-up version of a road bike anyone could buy."

"I fight for every inch out on the track."

Profile

Name:	Chaz Davies
Born:	10 February 1987 in Knighton, Powys
Lives:	Presteigne, Powys
Career:	Began racing in the Mini Moto championship in 1995 at eight years old. Made his adult racing debut in 1999 at just 12 years old.

Chaz Davies

Honours board

2001	Became youngest ever winner of a British Championship race, at 14
2002	Youngest ever rider in a GP Motorcycle racing season at 15
2008	Won the Daytona 200 – the first UK racer to win this prized title
2011	Won the World Supersport Championship and BBC Wales Sports Personality of the Year
2012	One win and four places on the winner's podium for his first year in Superbikes
2013	Won both Superbike-series races in Spain in April on a BMW bike

Mark Colbourne

Paralympic cyclist Mark Colbourne went to hell and back to win a gold and two silvers at the 2012 Olympics. Mark's win was a triumph of grit and determination following a terrible accident just three years previously.

Life changer

Mark was always mad on sport. As well as volleyball, he was a keen triathlete. But he believed his sporting career was over when he broke his back in a paragliding accident in 2009. "The worst thing in the world is when you've had something taken away from you and you have no control over it." It took a year of pain to walk again. Then in 2010 Disability Sport Wales put him on a track bike with stabilisers. "It just opened up a door for me. I realised there were opportunities for people like me." Mark put his all into training and became leaner, fitter and faster.

Did you know?

Mark broke the world record in the 3 km pursuit twice in one day at the 2012 Paralympics, shaving over 7 seconds off the record.

Mark's silver medal on 30 August was the first medal for Team GB at the 2012 Paralympics. It gave the whole team a boost!

Profile

Name:	Mark Colbourne
Born:	9 November 1969 in Tredegar, Blaenau Gwent / Monmouthshire
Lives:	Tredegar
Career:	A keen sportsman, Mark represented Wales in volleyball. But in 2009 he suffered a near-fatal paragliding accident which left him badly injured.

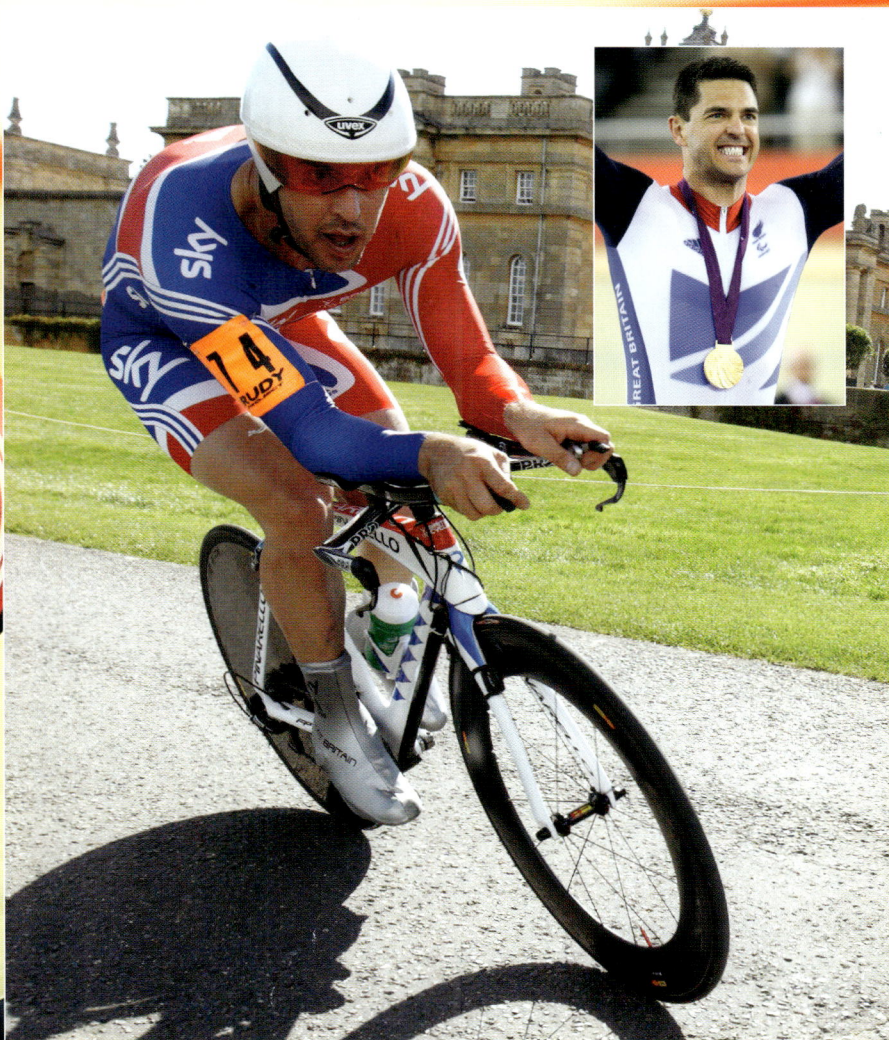

Big break: Paralympics 2012

30 August 2012 Took silver at C1 1 km time trial, shaving 3 seconds off his personal best

31 August 2012 Won gold at 3 km pursuit

5 September 2012 Won second silver at 6 km road time trial

Insider info

Mark competes in the C1 class in paracycling, for riders on upright bikes with the most severe disability

Honours board

2011   Won silver at C1 time trial at Road World Championships in Denmark

2011   Took gold in the C1 3 km pursuit and silver in the 1 km time trial at Para-Cycling Track World Championships in USA

2012   A gold and two silver medals at the 2012 Olympics

2013   Awarded MBE for services to sport

ROWING
Tom James

Overcoming health problems

As a schoolboy Tom was a keen runner. He took up rowing when a knee injury forced him to give up running. A further setback came in 2011, when doctors discovered he had a minor heart problem. He battled to be passed fit for competing.

Insider info

In rowing competitions, rowers compete singly or in teams of 2, 4 and 8. Teams of 8 always have a coxswain (cox) who steers. Pairs and fours may be coxed or coxless. Tom's favourite event is the coxless four.

Big break

Key races: 2008 and 2012 Olympics
Britain's main rivals in the coxless four are the Australians. In 2008 the Australians led almost all the way, but the British team pushed hard at the end, to cross the finish line just 1.28 seconds ahead. In 2012 Tom and his three crewmates edged ahead early on and held on to their lead to delight the mainly British crowd.

The rower from Wrexham has done the double, winning Olympic gold in the coxless four in 2008 and again in 2012. Now that's truly oarsome!

Profile

Name:	Tom James
Born:	11 March 1984 in Cardiff
Grew up:	Coed-poeth, near Wrexham
Lives:	Henley-on-Thames, England
Career:	At 18 Tom went to Cambridge University to study engineering. He graduated in 2007. Tom made his rowing debut for Great Britain in 2003, winning bronze in the men's eight at the World Championships.

Winning gold in 2012

"Whilst you're doing the race you're not really thinking about where you are, you're just racing, you're thinking about every stroke and what you can do to make it better… then you realise you've won."

Honours board

2008 Won gold medal in coxless four at the Olympics
2009 Awarded MBE
2011 Gold in coxless four at the World Championships
2012 Won second Olympic gold in coxless four at the London Olympics

"Having a tough opposition is what you want. It gets the best out of you and you really find something extra."

Did you know?

Tom competed in the Oxford vs Cambridge University Boat Race four times while at Cambridge. He lost the first three races but won his final race, where he was Cambridge President in 2007.

Leanda Cave

In 2012 triathlete Leanda Cave pulled off an amazing double. She won both the Ironman and Half-Ironman World Championships – two incredibly gruelling long-distance races. Triathlon events involve swimming, cycling and running.

In 2012 Leanda became the first woman to complete the amazing Ironman and Half-Ironman double, and only the second human being to do so. She said: "I've had some pretty big moments in my career and this is right up there."

Insider info

The Ironman is an incredibly gruelling triathlon race. It involves swimming 4 km, cycling 180 km and then running a marathon, 42 km. The Half-Ironman involves swimming, cycling and running exactly half that distance: a 2 km swim, a 90 km bike ride and a 21 km run. Both races are incredibly tough!

Profile

Name:	Leanda Cave
Born:	9 March 1978 in Louth, Lincolnshire
Grew up:	Australia, where her parents moved when she was four
Lives:	USA. With a Welsh mother, she chooses to race for Wales
Career:	Began running triathlons in 1994, aged 16. Went pro in 2000. Started competing over shorter courses and gradually increased to Ironman distance.

"This is the hardest race ever."

Big break

In 2002 Leanda won silver in triathlon at the Commonwealth Games and became World Triathlon Champion. However, these Olympic-distance races, over a total of 51 km, involve less than half the distance of a Half-Ironman and less than a quarter of the full Ironman! Over the next five years Leanda increased her stamina and distance to enable her to compete at Ironman level.

"I was never the best runner or the best swimmer or the best biker. But over the years with all the training and racing I've done, I feel that now I am one of those athletes who has talent."

Did you know?

Growing up in Australia, Leanda was a surf lifeguard and ran cross-country. Her sister, another triathlete, encouraged her to enter her first race.

Honours board

2002 Became World Triathlon Champion
2008 Won her first Ironman and also Escape from Alcatraz race, held in California – she has now won this race three times
2012 Won both Ironman and Half-Ironman World Championships. Nominated for Welsh Sports Personality of the Year

Nathan Cleverly

> "You only achieve what you truly believe."

Nathan Cleverly packs a punch both in the ring and in his studies. The world light-heavyweight boxing champ gained a maths degree in 2010.

Insider info: Boxing Cleverly?

Nathan trained hard as a pro boxer while completing his studies at Cardiff University. "As well as crunching numbers to gain a maths degree, I've had to fight for the British, Commonwealth and European titles as well, and spend most evenings hitting the heavy bag and doing press-ups and sit-ups." He graduated from Cardiff University in 2010.

Did you know?

At school Nathan excelled at sport. A talented footballer, he also won the under-15s Welsh cross-country championship.

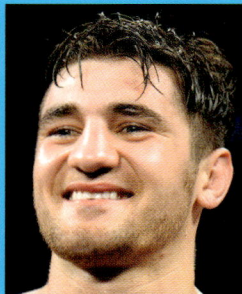

Profile

Name: Nathan Cleverly

Born: 17 February 1987 in Caerphilly

Career: Won 36 out of 36 amateur fights before turning pro in 2007. After winning the Commonwealth, British and European Light-Heavyweight titles he became World Boxing Organization (WBO) Light Heavyweight Champion in 2011.

Nathan has successfully defended his WBO title four times, against Tony Bellew in 2011, Tommy Karpency and Shawn Hawk in 2012 and Robin Krasniqi in 2013. He managed to gain an unbeaten run of 26 wins in 26 fights including 12 knock-outs.

Inspiration: Joe Calzaghe

Nathan originally trained with Joe Calzaghe in Newport. Known as the "Pride of Wales", Calzaghe was WBO Super-Middleweight Champion and The Ring Light-Heavyweight Champion. He is the longest-reigning world champion of recent years, successfully defending his Super-Middleweight title 21 times. He held the title for over ten years before retiring unbeaten in 2009.

Big break

In 2011 Nathan became the first Welshman to have won the British, Commonwealth, European and World titles since Freddie Welsh, the "Welsh Wizard", in the 1910s.

Honours board

2008 Won Commonwealth Light-Heavyweight title with points victory over Tony Oakey

2008 Won British Light-Heavyweight title by defeating Danny McIntosh

2010 Took European title by knocking out Antonio Brancalion

2010 Won Boxing Writers' Young Boxer of the Year Award

2011 Awarded full WBO Light-Heavyweight belt and defended it against Aleksy Kuziemski

2012 Nominated for Welsh Sports Personality of the Year

Josie Pearson

> "I have always been very determined. I have always wanted to be the best in my sport."

Did you know?
Wheelchair rugby is so vicious it is known as murderball! Josie was the first British woman to compete in wheelchair rugby in the Paralympics.

Profile

Name:	Josie Pearson
Born:	3 January 1986 in Bristol
Lives:	Hay-on-Wye, Powys
Career:	Competed in five events: show-jumping, dressage riding, wheelchair rugby, wheelchair racing and club throwing before winning gold in the discus.

All-round athlete Josie Pearson fought back from a terrible car crash to win gold for the discus throw at the 2012 Paralympics.

Life changer

A keen horserider, Josie showed promise as a show-jumper. But a terrible road accident in 2003 left her in a wheelchair with a damaged spine. At Oswestry Spinal Unit she met Alan Ash, who had a similar injury. Alan was a keen wheelchair rugby player and persuaded Josie to try it. She ended up competing in the mixed-sex sport at the 2008 Paralympics. But the team was just beaten to a medal, finishing fourth.

Insider info

In 2009 Josie switched from rugby to wheelchair racing, but quit when she realised the sport was doing further damage to her neck. She then took up club throwing and finally discus, to win gold in the F521 category.

Big break

Josie's main rivals in the 2012 discus were Catherine O'Neill from Ireland and Zena Cole from the USA. Josie broke the world record three times in her first three throws! She won gold with a huge margin of 242 points. O'Neill got the silver and Cole the bronze.

Inspiration: Aled Sion Davies

Fellow Welsh athlete Aled Sion Davies also shone at the 2012 Paralympics. He won gold in the F42 discus and bronze in the F42/44 shot put. Aled was born with a disability which affects his right leg. He trained for years without funding, and delayed going to university before finally getting a sponsor. He is now aiming for gold at the 2014 Commonwealth Games.

HURDLING
Dai Greene

Did you know?
While still at school Dai was a talented footballer. He played for Swansea City youth squad and scored a penalty against Real Madrid's youth side. But he turned down the chance to become a pro footballer at 16.

Did you know?
Dai once funded his athletics training by working at McDonald's.

Profile

Name:	Dai Greene
Born:	11 April 1986 in Felin-foel, Carmarthenshire
Sports:	400 m, 400 m hurdles
Career:	Showed early promise as a footballer but gave it up for athletics. In 2007 he won gold in the European Athletics Junior Championships 400 m hurdles before competing as a senior.
	With a personal best of 47.84 seconds, Dai is the second fastest Briton over the 400 m hurdles after Kriss Akabusi, who set the record in 1992.

Guts and determination are key strengths of champion 400 m hurdler Dai Greene. These qualities led to him being chosen as captain for GB's athletics squad in 2012.

"When I step on the start line I know I have prepared better than anyone. I do the best I can to be in the best shape possible."

Health setbacks

Dai gave up football after suffering a knee problem that affects young people during growth spurts. He has had knee surgery several times. At 17 doctors discovered he had epilepsy, a condition that causes fits. Dai uses a strict diet and training to control the condition. He says: "I can't think of a single reason why epilepsy would stop me winning a medal."

Heroes

When he was growing up Dai's hero was Wales and Manchester United footballer Ryan Giggs. Giggs is the most decorated player in English football history. As a boy Dai trained himself to use his left foot like Giggs. This proved useful when he became a hurdler. Dai's other hero is 110 m hurdler Colin Jackson, who was three times World Champion and won silver at the 1988 Olympics.

Honours board

2009 Silver in the 4 x 400 m relay in the World Championships
2010 Gold in 400 m hurdles at the European Athletics Championships, and gold at the Commonwealth Games
2011 Gold at World Athletics Championships

Olympic agony

Going into the 2012 Olympics Dai was tipped for gold. But he finished fourth in the 4 x 400 m relay and fourth in the 400 m hurdles. On both occasions he lost out on a medal by just three-tenths of a second.

CYCLING

Becky James

Cycling is in the blood in the James family. Becky's older sister Rachel, and younger sisters Ffion and Megan, are all keen cyclists.

Did you know?

While still at school Becky took part in an off-road cycling contest on her mum's bike. She came last – the event probably triggered a gritty will to win!

Did you know?

After winning four medals at the World Championships in 2013 Becky had to hitch a lift back to the hotel after the GB team forgot her! The BBC sports team came to the rescue and gave her a ride.

Becky's favourite food is iced cupcakes! While at school she used to work in a bakery in Abergavenny. She still loves baking.

Profile

Name:	Rebecca Angharad James
Born:	29 November 1991 in Abergavenny, Monmouthshire
Career:	Began competing in 2005. Becky won gold and set a new world record for the 200 m sprint as a junior. She went pro in 2010.

In 2013 Becky James became the only British cyclist ever to win four medals at a single World Championship. The biker from Abergavenny is tipped as cycling's new star.

Insider info

In 2013 Becky became world champion in the sprint and keirin. The keirin is a track race in which cyclists sprint for the finish after following a bike or motorbike that sets the pace in the opening stages. The world champion is always given a multicoloured rainbow jersey which she or he has to wear in the next race.

Big break

Becky hoped to take part in the 2012 Olympics but illness and injury kept her out. She soon got over her disappointment, and focused on the next challenge. "I love the sport and if you love it you'll get over it and focus on the next thing ahead." Her commitment paid off in 2013 when she scooped four medals at the World Championships in Minsk, Belarus. "It's absolutely crazy," she said of her historic win.

Training tips

Before a race Becky does her cycling warm-up while listening to electronic dance music. She chooses reggae and reggae fusion to get herself in the mood for winning.

Honours board

2010 Won silver for the sprint and bronze in the 500 m time trial in the Commonwealth Games
2010 Nominated for BBC Wales Sports Personality of the Year award
2013 Two golds in the sprint and keirin, and two bronzes in the team sprint and 500 m time trial in the World Championships in Minsk

Quiz

Have you got what it takes to be a sports star?

Have you got the makings of a top athlete? Find out by taking our quiz.

1. To make it to the very top you need a strong drive to win. Are you competitive when you play sport?

    a. It's first or nothing as far as I'm concerned. I play to win.

    b. I don't enjoy being beaten but you can't come first every time.

    c. I'm not bothered about coming first. My motto is "It's not winning but taking part that counts".

2. Top sportspeople give up everything to spend long, hard hours training. Have you got the dedication to put in the work?

    a. Long hours of training are no problem – sport comes first for me.

    b. I don't mind regular training but other things are important too.

    c. There's no way I am giving up everything to train every day.

3. To succeed at sport takes natural ability as well as grit and determination. How would you rate your skills at your favourite sport?

    a. I'm lucky – I seem to come first or second every time without a lot of effort.

    b. I'm in the top five but not always first.

    c. I'm no champion – my skills are average, though I love playing sport.

4. Top athletes need to be in peak condition. How would you rate your fitness?

    a. I maintain a peak level of fitness so I can always give my best.

    b. I'm fairly fit but a tough training session is pretty tiring.

    c. Not great. I struggle to stay fit enough to keep up with everyone else.

Answers

Mostly a: You have what it takes to be a champion: skill, fitness, dedication and the will to win.

Mostly b: Your skill and fitness are good, but you probably need to push yourself a bit harder to get to the top.

Mostly c: You don't seem to care enough to be a top sportsperson, but perhaps you just haven't found the right sport.

Glossary

Altitude	the height above sea level.
Category	a division within a group or class.
Commitment	when a person dedicates himself or herself to something.
Compete	to take part in a sport or enter a competition, with the aim of winning. Someone who competes is called a competitor.
Cox	short for coxswain, the person who steers a boat.
Debut	the first time a person, such as an athlete, appears in public.
Dressage	a competition for horse-riders, in which the horse is guided to carry out a series of movements.
Dwarfism	when an adult is unusually short, less than 147 cm (58 in) tall.
Epilepsy	a health problem in which the person suffers fits.
Excel	when someone does very well at something.
Flanker	a sportsperson positioned on the side, where he or she can receive the ball.
Graduate	when a person gains an academic degree or diploma.
Marathon	a long-distance foot race.
Paralympian	an athlete with a disability who takes part in the Paralympics, a series of international competitions for disabled athletes.
Patronise	to support a person or organisation, but also when someone talks to you in a condescending way.
Podium	the platform on which the winners of a competition stand to receive their medals or trophies.
Pro	short for professional. When someone turns pro he or she becomes a professional in a sport in which he / she previously took part as an amateur, for fun.
rsue	to follow.
odel	a successful person, such as an athlete, who inspires others.
per	the captain of a ship or team, or to captain a ship or team.
onsor	a company or wealthy person who provides money or equipment to a sportsperson, so he or she can compete in sport.
Taekwondo	a martial art in which athletes score points by striking with the feet and fists.
Triathlete	an athlete who competes in a triathlon, which involves three sports: swimming, cycling and running.